Table of contents
For
The Wellness Blueprint

Chapter 1: Nutrition

-The basics of healthy eating
-The role of nutrition in maintaining good health
-The importance of whole foods
-The benefits of a plant-based diet
-Creating a balanced meal plan
-Common nutrition myths and fads
-Practical tips for eating out and staying on track

Chapter 2: Fitness

-The importance of regular physical activity
-The benefits of different types of exercise
-Creating an exercise routine that works for you
-Common fitness myths

-Tips for staying motivated and overcoming

obstacles

Chapter 3: Mental Health

-The importance of mental health
-Common mental health conditions
-Practical tips for managing stress and improving emotional well-being

-The importance of self-care and therapy

Chapter 4: Sleep

-The importance of sleep
-The effects of poor sleep on the body and mind
-Creating a sleep-conducive environment

-Practical tips for improving sleep hygiene

Chapter 5: Self-care

-The importance of self-care
-Different forms of self-care
-Practical tips for incorporating self-care practices into daily life

-The importance of mindfulness and

self-compassion

Chapter 01   Nutrition

The basics of healthy eating

The basics of healthy eating involve consuming a balanced and varied diet that includes a variety of nutrient-dense foods. This includes a variety of fruits, vegetables, whole grains, lean proteins, and healthy fats.

- Fruits and vegetables: These provide important vitamins, minerals, and antioxidants that support overall health. Aim for at least 5 servings of fruits and vegetables per day.
- Whole grains: Whole grains are a good source of fiber and provide important nutrients such as B vitamins, iron, and magnesium. Whole grains include whole

wheat, oats, quinoa, barley, and brown rice.

- Lean proteins: Proteins are important for building and repairing muscle, and maintaining healthy skin and hair. Good sources of lean protein include fish, poultry, lean beef, tofu, and legumes.
- Healthy fats: Fats are an important source of energy and essential for maintaining healthy cell growth and development. Healthy fats include olive oil, avocado, nuts, and seeds.
- Hydration: It is important to stay hydrated by drinking enough water throughout the day.

It is also important to limit your intake of processed foods, added sugars, and saturated fats. Additionally, it's important to be mindful of portion sizes and to listen to your body's hunger and fullness cues.

It's important to note that everyone's dietary needs are different, and it's important to consult with a healthcare provider or a registered dietitian before making any major changes to your diet. With the right approach and personalized plan, you can improve your nutrition and enjoy the benefits of good health.

The role of nutrition in maintaining good health

The role of nutrition in maintaining good health is vital. Proper nutrition is essential for maintaining optimal physical and mental health and can prevent a wide range of chronic diseases. A well-balanced diet can provide the body with the necessary energy, nutrients, and fluids to sustain overall health and well-being.

- Adequate nutrition supports growth and development, particularly in children and adolescents.
- Proper nutrition can improve cardiovascular health by maintaining healthy cholesterol and blood pressure levels.
- A well-balanced diet can also improve immune function, making the body more resistant to infections and illnesses.
- Eating a diet rich in fruits, vegetables, and whole grains is associated with a lower risk of certain types of cancer.

- Proper nutrition can also improve mental health and cognitive function.
- Adequate nutrition is important for maintaining healthy skin, hair, and nails.
- Good nutrition also plays a role in maintaining a healthy weight and preventing obesity.
- Proper nutrition is also essential for maintaining bone health, and can prevent bone-related conditions such as osteoporosis.
- It's important to note that everyone's nutritional needs are different and it's important to consult with a healthcare provider or a registered dietitian before making any major changes to your diet. With the right approach and personalized plan, you can improve your

nutrition and enjoy the benefits of good health.

The   importance of whole foods

Whole foods refer to foods that are minimally processed and retain most of their natural nutritional value. Whole foods include fruits, vegetables, whole grains, lean proteins, and healthy fats. These foods are generally free from added sugars, preservatives, and artificial ingredients, and are a much healthier option compared to processed foods.

- Eating whole foods can help to reduce the risk of chronic diseases such as heart disease, type 2 diabetes and some cancers.

- Whole foods are rich in essential nutrients and antioxidants that support overall health and well-being.
- Whole foods are also a good source of fiber, which is essential for maintaining a healthy gut and preventing constipation.
- Whole foods can also help with weight management, as they tend to be more filling and satisfying than processed foods.
- Whole foods are also beneficial for maintaining healthy skin, hair, and nails.
- Whole foods are often lower in calories, which can help with weight management and weight loss.
- Whole foods also provide a variety of flavors, textures, and colors that can

make meals more enjoyable and satisfying.

- It's important to note that not all whole foods are created equal and it's important to choose nutrient-dense options, such as leafy greens, berries, and fatty fish, to ensure you're getting the most nutritional value. Eating a diet rich in whole foods can be a great way to improve your overall health, and prevent chronic diseases.

The benefits of a plant based diet

A plant-based diet is a diet that primarily consists of foods derived from plants, such as fruits, vegetables, whole grains, legumes, nuts, and seeds. It is a diet that is low in saturated fats, cholesterol and animal protein, and high in fiber, vitamins, and minerals.

- Plant-based diets have been shown to reduce the risk of chronic diseases such as heart disease, type 2 diabetes, and certain types of cancer.

- Plant-based diets are typically high in antioxidants, which can help to protect the body against cell damage and reduce the risk of disease.

- Plant-based diets are also high in fiber which can help to lower cholesterol levels and improve gut health.

- Plant-based diets are often lower in calories, which can help with weight management and weight loss.

- Plant-based diets are also beneficial for the environment, as the production of plant-based foods generally requires less land, water, and other resources.
- Plant-based diets can also be more sustainable in the long term, as they are often easier to stick to than restrictive diets.

It's important to note that a plant-based diet can be beneficial for health, but it's important to ensure you're consuming a variety of nutrient-dense plant-based foods and that you're meeting your nutritional needs. Some plant-based foods may lack certain essential nutrients, such as vitamin B12, which is primarily found in animal products. It's important to consult with a healthcare provider or a registered dietitian before making any major changes to your diet.

Creating a balanced meal plan

Creating a balanced meal plan involves selecting a variety of nutrient-dense foods that provide the body with the necessary energy, nutrients, and fluids to sustain overall health and well-being. Here are some tips for creating a balanced meal plan:

- Start by making a list of nutrient-dense foods that you enjoy eating. These can include fruits, vegetables, whole grains, lean proteins, and healthy fats.

- Plan your meals and snacks in advance. This can help you to ensure that you're getting the necessary nutrients throughout the day.

- Make sure to include a variety of different foods in your meals and snacks. Eating a variety of different foods will help to ensure that you're getting a wide range of essential nutrients.

- Incorporate colorful fruits and vegetables into your meals, as these foods are often high in essential vitamins, minerals, and antioxidants.

- Include a source of lean protein at each meal, such as fish, poultry, lean beef, tofu, or legumes.

- Include healthy fats at meals and snacks, such as avocado, nuts, and seeds.

- Limit your intake of processed foods, added sugars, and saturated fats.

- Be mindful of portion sizes and listen to your body's hunger and fullness cues.

- Consult with a healthcare provider or a registered dietitian before making any major changes to your diet.

It's important to note that everyone's dietary needs are different and that a balanced meal plan will differ from one person to another. Consult with a healthcare provider or a registered dietitian to create a personalized meal plan that suits your individual needs.

Common nutrition myths and fad

There are many nutrition myths and fads that can be misleading and can lead to confusion when trying to make healthy dietary choices. Here are some common nutrition myths and fads:

- Carbohydrates are bad for you: Carbs are essential for providing energy to the body and should be included in a healthy diet. Whole grains, fruits, vegetables, and legumes are all good sources of carbohydrates.
- Fat-free or low-fat foods are always healthier: Fat-free or low-fat foods often contain added sugar to make up for the

lack of flavor. It's important to choose nutrient-dense sources of healthy fats, such as avocado, nuts, and seeds.

- Eating at night will make you gain weight: The timing of your meals does not affect weight gain, it's the total number of calories consumed that matters.

- Gluten-free diets are healthier: Unless you have celiac disease or gluten intolerance, there is no evidence that avoiding gluten is healthier for the general population.

- Detox diets and juice cleanses are necessary for weight loss and overall health: The body is capable of detoxifying itself and these diets can be low in essential nutrients and may be harmful if followed for an extended period of time.

- Supplements can replace a healthy diet: Supplements can be beneficial in certain situations, but they should not be used to replace a healthy diet.

It's important to be skeptical of any diet or nutrition claims that seem too good to be true, and to consult with a healthcare provider or registered dietitian before making any major changes to your diet.

Practical tips for eating out and staying on track

Eating out can make it challenging to maintain a healthy diet, but it is possible to make healthy choices even when dining out. Here are some practical tips for eating out and staying on track:

- Plan ahead: Look up the menu online before you go and decide on a healthy option in advance.
- Ask for modifications: Many restaurants are willing to accommodate special requests such as using less oil or butter, or substituting steamed vegetables for fries.
- Share a meal: Many restaurant portions are quite large, so consider sharing a meal or taking half of it home for later.

- Make smart substitutions: When ordering, opt for whole wheat bread, brown rice, or whole wheat pasta instead of white.

- Be mindful of dressings and sauces: Dressings and sauces can add a lot of extra calories, so ask for them on the side and use them sparingly.

- Stay hydrated: Drink water with your meal and avoid sugary drinks.

- Be mindful of your portion sizes: Be mindful of how much you are eating and listen to your body's hunger and fullness cues.

- Don't feel guilty: If you do end up indulging, don't beat yourself up about it. Just make sure to get back on track at your next meal.

Remember that eating out should be enjoyable, and that small changes can make a big impact in maintaining a healthy diet. It's also important to consult with a healthcare provider or a registered dietitian before making any major changes to your diet.

Chapter 2 Fitness

-The importance of regular physical activity

Regular physical activity is essential for maintaining good health and well-being. It has numerous physical and mental health benefits, including:

- Improving cardiovascular health by strengthening the heart and lungs and reducing the risk of heart disease, stroke, and high blood pressure.

- Strengthening muscles and bones, which can help prevent osteoporosis and falls.
- Improving flexibility and balance, which can help to prevent injuries and falls.
- Enhancing mood and reducing stress and anxiety.
- Improving sleep quality.
- Helping with weight management and weight loss.
- Improving overall quality of life.

The American Heart Association recommends at least 150 minutes of moderate-intensity aerobic activity or 75 minutes of vigorous-intensity aerobic activity, or a combination of both, per week for adults. Additionally, adults should also engage in muscle-strengthening activities at least two days a week.

It's important to note that everyone's physical activity needs are different and that it's important to consult with a healthcare provider before starting a new exercise program. With the right approach and personalized plan, you can incorporate regular physical activity into your life and enjoy the many benefits it has to offer.

-The benefits of different types of exercise

There are many different types of exercise, each with their own unique benefits. Here are some of the most common types of exercise and their benefits:

- Aerobic exercise: Also known as cardio, aerobic exercise is any activity that increases the heart rate and breathing. Examples include jogging, cycling, swimming, and dancing. Aerobic exercise can improve cardiovascular health, increase lung capacity, and boost the immune system.
- Strength training: Strength training exercises target specific muscle groups and use resistance to build muscle mass. Examples include weightlifting, bodyweight exercises, and resistance band exercises. Strength training can improve muscle and bone health,

increase metabolism, and improve posture.

- Flexibility and stretching: Flexibility exercises, such as yoga and stretching, improve range of motion and reduce the risk of injury. They also can help improve posture and reduce muscle tension and soreness.

- Balance and coordination: Activities that improve balance and coordination, such as tai chi, can help prevent falls and improve overall stability.

- High-intensity interval training (HIIT): HIIT is a type of cardio that alternates short bursts of intense activity with periods of recovery. This type of exercise can be very effective for weight loss and improving cardiovascular fitness.

- Mind-body exercises: Mind-body exercises, such as yoga and Pilates, combine physical movement with mindfulness and breathing exercises. These exercises can help reduce stress and anxiety and improve overall well-being.

It's important to note that everyone's exercise needs are different and that it's important to consult with a healthcare provider before starting a new exercise program. With the right approach and personalized plan, you can incorporate different types of exercise into your life and enjoy the many benefits they have to offer.

Creating an exercise routine that works for you

Creating an exercise routine that works for you involves finding activities that you enjoy and that fit your lifestyle. Here are some steps to help you create an effective exercise routine:

1. Set specific, measurable goals for yourself. Examples include "I want to run a 5K" or "I want to be able to do 10 push-ups."
2. Assess your current fitness level. This will help you determine what types of exercise are appropriate for you and how much you should be doing.

3. Create a schedule. Decide on the days and times that you will exercise each week, and make sure to stick to it.

4. Mix it up. Incorporate a variety of activities into your routine to prevent boredom and to work different muscle groups.

5. Get a workout partner. Having someone to exercise with can help keep you motivated and accountable.

6. Be consistent. Regular exercise is key to achieving your goals.

7. Keep in mind that it's important to listen to your body and adjust your routine as needed. If you're feeling tired or achy, take it easy and try to rest.

8. Remember to consult a doctor or a personal trainer to get professional

advice and guidance that suit your specific needs and goals.

Common fitness myths

There are many fitness myths that circulate in the fitness industry. Here are a few common ones:

1. "No pain, no gain": While exercise should be challenging, it should not be painful. If an exercise is causing pain, stop and seek advice from a trainer or doctor.
2. "Muscle turns into fat if you stop working out": Muscle and fat are two different types of tissue, so one cannot turn into the other. However, if you stop

working out and start eating more, you may gain weight in the form of fat.

3. "Crunches will give you a six-pack": Crunches are an effective exercise for working the abdominal muscles, but they will not give you a six-pack if you have a layer of fat covering them. To see your abs, you need to lose body fat through a combination of diet and cardio exercise.

4. "Stretching before exercise prevents injury": While stretching can help improve flexibility, it does not prevent injury. In fact, static stretching before exercise can actually decrease performance.

5. "You can target specific areas of your body to lose fat": There is no such thing

as spot reduction. Losing fat from a specific area of your body requires overall weight loss through a combination of diet and exercise.

6. "You should exercise every day": Your body needs rest and recovery time to repair and grow. It's important to give your body at least one day of rest a week, and to listen to your body if it's telling you that you need more rest.

7. "Cardio is the best way to lose weight": While cardio is great for burning calories, strength training is also important for weight loss. Building muscle can boost your metabolism and increase the number of calories you burn at rest.

8. "You can't eat after a certain time of day": The timing of your meals is less important than the total number of calories you consume. Eating a meal late at night will not necessarily cause you to gain weight, as long as you stay within your calorie needs for the day.

Tips for staying motivated and overcoming obstacles

Staying motivated and overcoming obstacles are important parts of achieving your fitness goals. Here are some tips that may help:

1. Set specific, measurable goals: Having a clear goal in mind will help you stay motivated and focused.

2. Keep a workout journal: Tracking your progress can help you see how far you've come and stay motivated.

3. Find an accountability partner: Having someone to share your goals and progress with can help you stay on track.

4. Reward yourself: Set small rewards for yourself when you achieve certain milestones.

5. Find an activity you enjoy: If you enjoy the activity, you're more likely to stick with it.

6. Make it a habit: The more you make exercise a part of your daily routine, the easier it will be to stick to it.

7. Don't be too hard on yourself: It's normal to have setbacks and obstacles. Don't let them discourage you. Instead, use them as an opportunity to learn and grow.

8. Be flexible: Be open to trying new things and be willing to make adjustments to your routine as needed.

9. Remind yourself why you started: When you're feeling unmotivated, remind yourself of your reasons for starting this journey and how far you've come.

10. Get professional help if needed: If you're struggling to stay motivated, consider working with a personal trainer or a

therapist who can help you develop strategies for overcoming obstacles and staying on track.

Chapter 3:   Mental Health

The importance of mental health

Mental health is an important aspect of overall well-being and it plays a crucial role in how we think, feel and behave. Good mental health allows us to realize our full potential, cope with the normal stresses of life, work productively and make meaningful contributions to our communities.

1. Positive mental health enables us to:
- build and maintain healthy relationships
- make informed and responsible decisions

- adapt to change and uncertainty
- develop and maintain a sense of purpose and meaning in life

2. Poor mental health can lead to:

- depression, anxiety, and other mental illnesses
- substance abuse and addiction
- relationship problems
- poor work performance and unemployment
- physical health problems

3. Taking care of mental health is just as important as taking care of physical health. Some ways to take care of your mental health include:

- getting regular exercise
- eating a healthy diet
- getting enough sleep

- managing stress through relaxation techniques such as yoga, meditation, or deep breathing
- building and maintaining a support network of friends and family
- talking to a therapist or counselor if you need additional support
- seeking help if you think you might have a mental health condition

4. Remember that seeking help for mental health is a sign of strength, not weakness. It is important to take care of your mental health in order to live a happy, healthy and fulfilling life.

Common mental health conditions

There are many different mental health conditions that can affect people of all ages, genders, and backgrounds. Here are a few common ones:

1. Depression: a persistent feeling of sadness, loss of interest in things, and a lack of energy. It can affect sleep, appetite, and the ability to concentrate.

2. Anxiety: excessive worry and fear about everyday situations. It can manifest in different forms such as Generalized Anxiety Disorder, Panic Disorder, Social Anxiety Disorder, Specific Phobias.

3. Post-Traumatic Stress Disorder (PTSD): a condition that can develop after someone has been through a traumatic event such as a car accident, natural

disaster, or military combat. Symptoms include flashbacks, nightmares, and feelings of guilt or shame.

4. Bipolar disorder: characterized by extreme mood swings, from manic or hypomanic episodes (such as feeling high, having racing thoughts, and being easily distracted) to depressive episodes (such as feeling low, having little energy and interest in things).

5. Schizophrenia: a serious mental disorder characterized by a range of symptoms such as hallucinations, delusions, and disordered thinking.

6. Eating disorders: a group of conditions characterized by an abnormal attitude towards food that causes someone to change their eating habits and behavior.

The most common eating disorders are Anorexia Nervosa, Bulimia Nervosa, and Binge Eating Disorder.

7. Attention-deficit/hyperactivity disorder (ADHD): a condition characterized by inattention, hyperactivity, and impulsivity.

8. Obsessive-compulsive disorder (OCD): characterized by persistent, uncontrollable thoughts (obsessions) and repetitive behaviors (compulsions) that are intended to alleviate the anxiety caused by the obsessions.

It's important to note that many people may experience symptoms of mental health conditions, but that doesn't necessarily mean they have a diagnosable condition. If you are experiencing symptoms that concern you, it is important to speak with a mental health professional to receive a proper diagnosis and treatment plan.

Practical tips for managing stress and improving emotional well-being

Managing stress and improving emotional well-being are important for maintaining good mental health. Here are some practical tips that may help:

1. Exercise regularly: Exercise is a natural way to reduce stress and improve mood. Aim for at least 30 minutes of moderate-intensity activity on most days of the week.

2. Get enough sleep: Adequate sleep is essential for both physical and mental well-being. Aim for 7-9 hours of sleep per night.

3. Eat a healthy diet: Eating a well-balanced diet can help improve mood and reduce stress.

4. Practice relaxation techniques: Techniques such as deep breathing, yoga, and meditation can help reduce stress and improve emotional well-being.

5. Connect with others: Spending time with friends and family, or even just talking to someone you trust, can be a great way to reduce stress and improve emotional well-being.

6. Take time for yourself: Make sure to set aside time each day to do something you enjoy, such as reading, listening to music, or taking a walk.

7. Practice gratitude: Take time each day to think about what you are grateful for.

8. Learn to manage your time: Time management can help reduce stress and improve emotional well-being by reducing feelings of being overwhelmed.

9. Seek professional help if needed: If you are struggling to manage stress and improve emotional well-being on your own, consider seeking help from a therapist or counselor.

10. Be kind to yourself: Don't be too hard on yourself, it's important to be patient and

compassionate with yourself when you're going through a difficult time.

It's important to remember that different strategies will work for different people, and it may take some experimentation to find what works best for you. It's also important to keep in mind that it's normal to feel stressed at times, but if it starts to interfere with your daily life, it's important to seek help.

The importance of self-care and therapy

Self-care and therapy are important for maintaining good mental health and well-being.

1. Self-care: Self-care refers to the activities and practices that individuals do deliberately in order to take care of their physical, mental and emotional health. It's about being mindful of the things that nourish your body, mind and soul, and making them a priority. Examples of self-care include getting enough sleep, eating a healthy diet, exercising regularly, practicing relaxation techniques, and taking time for yourself.

2. Therapy: Therapy is a form of treatment for mental health conditions and emotional difficulties. It can take many forms, such as individual counseling, group therapy, or family therapy. It provides a safe and confidential space for people to talk about their thoughts,

feelings, and experiences. Therapy can help people to better understand themselves and their problems, develop coping skills, and make positive changes in their lives.

3. Importance of self-care and therapy: Both self-care and therapy are important for promoting emotional well-being and mental health. Self-care helps individuals maintain good physical and mental health, preventing the deterioration of mental health, and promoting resilience. Therapy provides individuals with a safe and confidential space to talk about their thoughts and feelings, and helps individuals understand their problems better and develop coping skills.

4. Together, self-care and therapy can provide a powerful combination for improving mental health and emotional well-being. Self-care helps individuals maintain good physical and mental health, while therapy provides individuals with the tools and support they need to work through difficult emotions and make positive changes in their lives.

It's important to note that self-care and therapy are not mutually exclusive, and in many cases, combining them can be beneficial for people. It's also important to remember that self-care and therapy are not a one-time solution, but rather a continuous process that requires time and commitment to be effective.

Chapter 4: Sleep

The importance of sleep

Sleep is essential for physical and mental well-being. Adequate sleep is important for maintaining overall health and well-being, and a lack of sleep can have negative effects on the body and mind.

1. Physical health: Adequate sleep is important for maintaining physical health. During sleep, the body repairs and regenerates tissues, strengthens the immune system, and regulates hormones. A lack of sleep can increase the risk of developing chronic health conditions such as obesity, diabetes,

cardiovascular disease, and even certain types of cancer.

2. Mental health: Sleep plays a crucial role in maintaining mental health. Lack of sleep can lead to mood swings, irritability, and difficulty concentrating. Insomnia and other sleep disorders have been linked to depression, anxiety, and other mental health conditions.

3. Cognitive function: Sleep is important for cognitive function, including memory, learning, and problem-solving. A lack of sleep can impair cognitive function, making it difficult to concentrate, learn new information, and make decisions.

4. Safety: Sleep deprivation can lead to accidents and injuries. Drowsy driving is a major cause of car accidents and

other incidents, and lack of sleep can also increase the risk of falls and other accidents at home and at work.

5. Quantity and quality of sleep: The recommended amount of sleep for adults is 7-9 hours per night, but the quality of sleep is also important. A good night's sleep should be uninterrupted, and people should wake up feeling refreshed and alert.

6. Sleep hygiene: Maintaining good sleep hygiene is important for ensuring adequate sleep. This includes avoiding caffeine and nicotine close to bedtime, avoiding screen time before sleep, maintaining a consistent sleep schedule, and creating a comfortable sleep environment.

7. Sleep disorders: Some people may have a sleep disorder, such as insomnia or sleep apnea, which can affect the quality and quantity of sleep. If you have trouble sleeping, it's important to speak with a healthcare professional.

It's important to prioritize sleep and make it a priority. By getting the recommended amount of sleep and maintaining good sleep hygiene, people can improve their physical and mental health, cognitive function, and overall well-being.

The effects of poor sleep on the body and mind

Poor sleep can have a wide range of negative effects on both the body and mind. Here are some of the most common effects of poor sleep:

1. Physical health: Poor sleep is associated with a number of physical health problems, including an increased risk of obesity, diabetes, cardiovascular disease, and some types of cancer. Poor sleep can also weaken the immune system, making it more difficult for the body to fight off infections.
2. Mental health: Poor sleep is also associated with a number of mental health problems, including depression, anxiety, and other mood disorders.

Insomnia and other sleep disorders have been linked to a higher risk of suicide.

3. Cognitive function: Poor sleep can affect cognitive function, including memory, learning, and problem-solving. It can also lead to problems with attention and concentration.

4. Safety: Poor sleep can increase the risk of accidents and injuries, such as drowsy driving, falls, and other accidents at home and at work.

5. Hormonal balance: Poor sleep can disrupt the balance of hormones in the body, including the hormones that control hunger and metabolism. This can lead to weight gain and other health problems.

6. Immune system: Poor sleep can weaken the immune system, making it more difficult for the body to fight off infections.

7. Aging: Chronic poor sleep can accelerate the aging process and increase the risk of age-related diseases such as Alzheimer's disease.

8. Inflammation: poor sleep is associated with an increase in inflammation in the body, which can lead to a wide range of health problems, including chronic diseases.

9. Inadequate sleep can also lead to poor performance in work or school, and negatively impact relationships and daily activities.

It's important to prioritize sleep and make it a priority to get the recommended amount of sleep and maintain good sleep hygiene to avoid the negative effects of poor sleep on the body and mind. If you have trouble sleeping, it's important to speak with a healthcare professional to identify any underlying causes and develop a plan to improve sleep.

Creating a sleep-conducive environment

Creating a sleep-conducive environment is important for getting a good night's sleep. Here are some steps you can take to create a sleep-conducive environment:

1. Keep the bedroom dark, quiet, and cool. Use heavy curtains or blinds to block out light, and use earplugs or a white noise machine to block out noise. Aim for a room temperature of around 65 degrees Fahrenheit.

2. Make your bed comfortable. Invest in a good quality mattress, pillows, and bedding that feels comfortable to you.

3. Avoid using electronic devices before bedtime. The blue light emitted by electronic devices such as smartphones, tablets, and computers can interfere with the production of melatonin, a hormone that helps regulate sleep.

4. Establish a bedtime routine. Try to go to bed and wake up at the same time every

day. A consistent sleep schedule can help regulate your body's internal clock.

5. Avoid caffeine, nicotine, and alcohol close to bedtime. These substances can disrupt sleep and make it more difficult to fall asleep.

6. Avoid heavy meals and exercise close to bedtime. Eating a heavy meal or engaging in vigorous exercise can disrupt sleep and make it more difficult to fall asleep.

7. Create a relaxing atmosphere. Use soothing scents, soft lighting, and comfortable furniture to create a relaxing atmosphere in your bedroom.

8. Use a comfortable mattress and pillows. A comfortable mattress and pillows can help ensure a good night's sleep.

9. Keep your bedroom clean and organized. A clean and organized bedroom can help promote relaxation and reduce stress.

10. Consider using a natural sleep aid. Some people find that using a natural sleep aid, such as chamomile tea or melatonin supplements, can help improve sleep.

It's important to remember that everyone's sleep needs are different, and what works for one person may not work for another. Experiment with different strategies to find what works best for you, and don't be afraid to ask for help if you are having difficulty getting

Practical tips for improving sleep hygiene

Improving sleep hygiene is important for getting a good night's sleep. Here are some practical tips for improving sleep hygiene:

1. Stick to a consistent sleep schedule. Try to go to bed and wake up at the same time every day, even on weekends.

2. Create a relaxing bedtime routine. Develop a relaxing pre-sleep routine, such as reading a book, taking a bath or listening to calming music.

3. Keep the bedroom dark, quiet, and cool. Use heavy curtains or blinds to block out light, and use earplugs or a white noise machine to block out noise. Keep the

bedroom at a cool temperature, around 65 degrees Fahrenheit is ideal.

4. Avoid electronic devices before bedtime. The blue light emitted by electronic devices can interfere with the production of melatonin, a hormone that helps regulate sleep.

5. Avoid caffeine, nicotine, and alcohol close to bedtime. These substances can disrupt sleep and make it more difficult to fall asleep.

6. Avoid heavy meals and exercise close to bedtime. Eating a heavy meal or engaging in vigorous exercise can disrupt sleep and make it more difficult to fall asleep.

7. Create a comfortable sleeping environment. Use comfortable bedding

and pillows, and make sure the mattress is supportive.

8. Keep the bedroom clean and organized. A clean and organized bedroom can help promote relaxation and reduce stress.

9. Try relaxation techniques. Try techniques like deep breathing, yoga, or meditation to help you relax and fall asleep.

10. Consider using a natural sleep aid. Some people find that using a natural sleep aid, such as chamomile tea or melatonin supplements, can help improve sleep.

It's important to remember that everyone's sleep needs are different and it may take some experimentation to find what works best for you. If you are having difficulty sleeping, it's important to speak with a healthcare professional to identify any underlying causes and develop a plan to improve sleep.

Chapter 5: Self-care

The importance of self-care

Self-care is the practice of taking care of oneself in order to maintain physical, mental, and emotional well-being. It's about being mindful of the things that nourish your body, mind and soul and making them a priority. It's important because it can help prevent the deterioration of mental health and promote resilience.

1. Physical health: Self-care practices such as regular exercise, healthy eating, and getting enough sleep can help improve physical health and prevent chronic diseases.

2. Mental health: Self-care practices such as relaxation techniques, journaling, and mindfulness can help improve mental health and reduce the risk of developing mental health conditions.

3. Emotional well-being: Self-care practices such as setting boundaries, expressing gratitude, and engaging in activities that bring joy can help improve emotional well-being and reduce stress.

4. Resilience: Self-care practices can help build resilience by providing individuals with the tools and support they need to

cope with difficult situations and bounce back from adversity.

5. Productivity: Self-care practices can improve productivity by helping individuals to stay focused, motivated, and energized.

6. Relationship: Self-care practices can improve relationships by helping individuals to communicate effectively, manage stress, and maintain healthy boundaries.

7. Positive mindset: Regular self-care practices can help develop a positive mindset, which can help to increase happiness, reduce stress and improve overall well-being.

Self-care is not a one-time solution, but rather a continuous process that requires time and commitment to be effective. It's important to find self-care practices that work for you and make them a regular part of your routine. Remember that self-care is not selfish, it's essential for maintaining good physical and mental health and well-being.

Different forms of self-care

Self-care can take many forms, and what works for one person may not work for another. Here are some examples of different forms of self-care:

1. Physical self-care: This includes activities that promote physical health, such as regular exercise, healthy eating, and getting enough sleep.

2. Mental and emotional self-care: This includes activities that promote mental and emotional well-being, such as meditation, journaling, and therapy.

3. Social self-care: This includes activities that promote social connections and relationships, such as spending time with friends and family, or joining a group or club.

4. Spiritual self-care: This includes activities that promote spiritual well-being, such as prayer, meditation, or yoga.

5. Creative self-care: This includes activities that promote creativity, such as art, music, or writing.

6. Professional self-care: This includes activities that promote career development and job satisfaction, such as further education and professional development.

7. Environmental self-care: This includes activities that promote a healthy environment, such as recycling, reducing energy consumption, and eating organic food.

8. Self-compassion: This includes being kind and understanding towards yourself and being forgiving with yourself when you make mistakes.

It's important to remember that self-care should be individualized and tailored to meet one's unique needs. It's also important to make self-care a regular part of your life, not only when you are feeling overwhelmed. It's also important to try different forms of self-care and find what works best for you.

Practical tips for incorporating self-care practices into daily life

Incorporating self-care practices into daily life can be challenging, but it's important for maintaining good physical and mental health and well-being. Here are some practical tips for incorporating self-care practices into daily life:

1. Make self-care a priority: Make self-care a regular part of your daily routine, and schedule it like any other important task.

2. Create a self-care plan: Identify the self-care practices that work best for you, and create a plan to make them a regular part of your daily routine.

3. Start small: Incorporating self-care practices into daily life can be overwhelming, so start small and gradually increase the frequency and intensity of the practices.

4. Find what works best for you: Experiment with different forms of self-care and find what works best for you.

5. Be flexible: Be open to trying new things and be flexible in your approach.

6. Make it easy: Make self-care practices easy to access, for example, keep a journal by the bed, or have your yoga mat in the living room.

7. Use reminders: Set reminders for self-care activities on your phone or calendar.

8. Get support: Enlist the help of friends and family, or consider joining a self-care group for support and accountability.

9. Take a break: Remember to take a break from your regular routine and schedule some time for yourself.

10. Be kind to yourself: Remember to be kind and compassionate towards yourself, and don't be too hard on yourself if you miss a self-care activity.

It's important to remember that self-care should be individualized and tailored to meet one's unique needs. It's also important to make self-care a regular part of your life, not only when you are feeling overwhelmed. With these tips, it will be easier to incorporate self-care practices into your daily routine, and make it a habit that can lead to a healthier and happier life.

The importance of mindfulness and self-compassion

Mindfulness and self-compassion are important for maintaining good mental and emotional well-being.

1. Mindfulness: Mindfulness is the practice of being present and engaged in the current moment, without judgment. It is about being aware of one's thoughts, feelings, and surroundings in a non-judgmental way. Mindfulness can help to reduce stress, improve mental well-being, and increase emotional regulation.

2. Self-compassion: Self-compassion is the practice of being kind and understanding towards oneself and being forgiving with oneself when making mistakes. It's about treating oneself with the same kindness, care, and understanding that one would offer to a good friend. Self-compassion can help to reduce stress, improve mental

well-being, and increase emotional regulation.

3. Together, mindfulness and self-compassion can help individuals to better understand and manage their thoughts, feelings, and behaviors. Mindfulness can help individuals to focus on the present moment and identify patterns in their thinking, while self-compassion can help individuals to be kind and understanding towards themselves, which can lead to greater emotional regulation and overall well-being.

4. Mindfulness and self-compassion can also help to build resilience, which is the ability to cope with difficult situations and bounce back from adversity. When

people are more mindful and self-compassionate, they are better able to cope with stress and bounce back from difficult situations.

5. Mindfulness and self-compassion can also be beneficial for individuals who are struggling with mental health conditions such as anxiety and depression. Mindfulness and self-compassion practices can be used as a complement to therapy and medication to help reduce symptoms and improve overall well-being.

It's important to remember that incorporating mindfulness and self-compassion practices into daily life takes time and commitment, and it's important to make it a   regular part of your routine. It's also important to be kind and compassionate towards yourself, and not to be too hard on yourself if you miss a practice.

In conclusion, wellness is a holistic concept that encompasses physical, mental, and emotional well-being. To achieve wellness, it's important to maintain a balanced lifestyle, including regular exercise, healthy eating, and getting enough sleep. It's also important to prioritize self-care and make it a regular part of your daily routine. Mindfulness and self-compassion are important practices that can help to reduce stress, improve mental well-being, and increase emotional regulation.

Creating a sleep-conducive environment, maintaining good sleep hygiene, and getting the recommended amount of sleep are also important for overall well-being. If you have trouble sleeping, it's important to speak with a healthcare professional to identify any underlying causes and develop a plan to improve sleep.

Incorporating self-care practices into daily life can be challenging, but it's important for maintaining good physical and mental health and well-being. It's also important to find self-care practices that work for you and make them a regular part of your routine. Remember that self-care is not selfish, it's essential for maintaining good physical and mental health and well-being.

Remember that wellness is an ongoing journey and that it takes time and commitment to achieve. Be kind and compassionate towards yourself, and don't be too hard on yourself if you miss a practice. Seek help if you need it, and always remember the importance of balance in all aspects of your life.